AIR FRYER COOKBOOK for BEGINNERS

EASY AND DELICIOUS RECIPES THAT ANYONE CAN COOK AT HOME – FOR BEGINNERS AND ADVANCED USERS

Clean Eating
Publishing

TABLE OF CONTENTS:

CHAPTER 1: PORK RECIPES 6

    PORK CHOPS FAST 7
    CRISPY BREADED PORK CHOPS 9
    JAMAICAN JERK PORK CHOPS 11
    ITALIAN SAUSAGE WITH PEPPERS AND ONION 13
    AL PASTOR TACOS 15
    EASY BBQ PORK SHREDDED PIZZA 17
    EASY GREEK MEETBALLS 18
    MEATBALL PARM SUB 20

CHAPTER 2: POULTRY RECIPES 23

    CHICKEN FAJITA TAQUITOS 24
    CHICKEN NUGGETS 27
    MARINATED CHICKEN BREASTS 29
    HEALTHY BREAKFAST FRITTATA 32
    GLUTEN FREE CHICKEN 34
    GARLIC PARMESAN CHICKEN TENDER 36
    EASY CHICKEN MANCHURIAN 38
    BARBECUE CHICKEN 40

CHAPTER 3: MEAT RECIPES 43

    STEAK WITH GARLIC HERB AND BUTTER 44
    NEW YORK STRIP STEAK 46
    MOROCCAN MEATBALLS 49
    VENISON BURGERS 50
    TACO STUFFED AVOCADOS 52
    STEAK AND CHEESE SANDWICH 54
    BEEF WONTONS 56

CHAPTER 4: VEGETABLE RECIPES 60

    ZUCCHINI CURLY FRIES 61
    EASY ROASTED ASPARAGUS 63
    STUFFED MUSHROOMS 65
    ITALIAN RATATOUILLE 67
    ZUCCHINI FRITTERS 69

CRISPY GNOCCHI 70
CARROTS WITH TAHINI-LEMON SAUCE 71
MEDITERRANEAN VEGETABLES MEDLEY 73
GRILLED VEGGIES AND COUS COUS 75

CHAPTER 5: FISH & SEAFOOD RECIPES 78

COCONUT PRAWNS 79
CAJUN SALMON 81
HEALTHY AND TASTY FISHCAKES 83
FISH STICKS 85
EASY BREADED SHRIMP 87
SHRIMP SANDWICH WITH TARTAR SAUCE 88
MASALA FRIED FISH 90

CHAPTER 6: APPETIZERS & SNACK RECIPES 93

CORN NUTS 94
WONDERFUL TRUFFLE FRIES 96
MINI PEPPERS STUFFED WITH CHEESE AND SAUSAGE 98
PITA CHIPS 100
BUTTERFLIED SHRIMP WITH PINEAPPLE AND MANGO SALSA 102
STUFFING BALLS 105
TORTILLA CHIPS 107
SPECIAL LEMON PEPPER CHICKEN DRUMSTICK 109

© Copyright 2021 by Clean Eating Publishing All rights reserved.

The following Book is reproduced below with the goal of providing information that is as accurate and reliable as possible. Regardless, purchasing this Book can be seen as consent to the fact that both the publisher and the author of this book are in no way experts on the topics discussed within and that any recommendations or suggestions that are made herein are for entertainment purposes only. Professionals should be consulted as needed prior to undertaking any of the action endorsed herein.

This declaration is deemed fair and valid by both the American Bar Association and the Committee of Publishers Association and is legally binding throughout the United States. Furthermore, the transmission, duplication, or reproduction of any of the following work including specific information will be considered an illegal act irrespective of if it is done electronically or in print.

This extends to creating a secondary or tertiary copy of the work or a recorded copy and is only allowed with the express written consent from the Publisher. All additional right reserved.

The information in the following pages is broadly considered a truthful and accurate account of facts and as such, any inattention, use, or misuse of the information in question by the reader will render any resulting actions solely under their purview.

There are no scenarios in which the publisher or the original author of this work can be in any fashion deemed liable for any hardship or damages that may befall them after undertaking information described herein.

Additionally, the information in the following pages is intended only for informational purposes and should thus be thought of as universal. As befitting its nature, it is presented without assurance regarding its prolonged validity or interim quality. Trademarks that are mentioned are done without written consent and can in no way be considered an endorsement from the trademark holder.

CHAPTER 1:

PORK

RECIPES

PORK CHOPS FAST

Prep:10 mins
Cook:15 mins
Total:25 mins
Servings:4
Yield:4 servings

INGREDIENT

⅓ cup grated Parmesan
4 each boneless pork chops,
1/2-inch thick
1 pinch salt and ground black pepper to taste
1 egg
cheese
⅓ cup almond flour
½ teaspoon salt
¼ teaspoon pepper
¼ teaspoon garlic powder
1 serving avocado oil cooking spray

Directions

1

Season pork chops with salt and pepper on both sides.

2

Beat egg in a medium bowl. Mix Parmesan cheese, almond flour, 1/2 teaspoon salt, 1/4 teaspoon pepper, and garlic powder together in a second bowl.

3

Dip each pork chop in egg, then in Parmesan-flour mixture to coat. Place in the air fryer basket and spritz with avocado oil.

4

Cook in an air fryer at 375 degrees F (190 degrees C) until lightly browned, 8 to 10 minutes. Flip pork chops over, spritz with avocado oil and cook until pork is no longer pink in the center, 3 to 4 minutes more.

Nutritions:

Per Serving: 365 calories; protein 47.2g; carbohydrates 2.8g; fat 17.4g; cholesterol 158.9mg; sodium 515.6mg.

CRISPY BREADED PORK CHOPS

Prep time:
10 min
Cook time:
8 min
Total time:
18 min

Ingredients

1 pound boneless pork chops, 1/2-inch thick
1/2 teaspoon kosher salt
1/4 teaspoon black pepper
1/2 cup all-purpose flour
1 teaspoon garlic powder, divided
1 teaspoon onion powder, divided
2 large eggs
splash of water
1/3 cup seasoned Italian breadcrumbs
1/3 cup grated parmesan cheese, plus more for garnish
fresh chopped parsley, for garnish

DIRECTIONS:

1:
Season pork chops on both sides with the salt and pepper, set aside.

2:
Set up your breading station with 3 shallow bowls:
Bowl 1: whisk together the flour, 1/2 teaspoon of garlic powder, and 1/2 teaspoon of the onion powder.
Bowl 2: thoroughly whisk together the eggs, splash of water, 1/2 teaspoon of the garlic powder, and 1/2 teaspoon of the onion powder.
Bowl 3: mix together the breadcrumbs and parmesan cheese.

3:
Place the pork chops one by one into the flour mixture and evenly coat. Shake off any excess flour and immediately place into the egg mixture, evenly coat. Let any excess egg drip off the pork chop and immediately place it into the breadcrumb mixture and evenly coat, shake off any excess. Repeat with the remaining pork chops.

4:
If your air fryer requires preheating, set it to 400°F for 5 minutes.

5:
Spray the air fryer basket with cooking spray; place two pork chops in the basket or as many as you can fit without them touching. Spray the tops of the pork chops with cooking spray.

6:
Air fry for 4 minutes, turn them over, spray the top with more cooking spray and air fry an additional 4 minutes or until an internal temperature reaches 145°F.

7:
Serve with a garnish of parsley and more grated parmesan, if desired.

NUTRITIONS:

Calories: 347kcal | Carbohydrates: 20g | Protein: 34g | Fat: 13g |

JAMAICAN JERK PORK CHOPS

Total Time
Prep/Total Time: 25 min.

Makes
2 servings

INGREDIENTS:

1 tablespoon butter, softened
1/4 cup peach preserves
4 boneless thin-cut pork loin chops (2 to 3 ounces each)
3 teaspoons Caribbean jerk seasoning
1/2 teaspoon salt
1/4 teaspoon pepper
1/2 medium sweet orange pepper
1/2 medium sweet yellow pepper
1/2 medium sweet red pepper

DIRECTIONS:

1
Preheat air fryer to 350°. In a small bowl, mix butter and peach preserves until combined; set aside.

2
Sprinkle chops with seasonings. Place on greased tray in air-fryer basket. Cook until no longer pink, 2-3 minutes on each side. Remove and keep warm.

3
Cut peppers into thin strips. Place on greased tray in air-fryer basket. Cook until crisp-tender and lightly browned, 5-6 minutes, stirring occasionally. Return chops to air fryer; top with butter mixture. Cook until butter is melted, 1-2 minutes. If desired, serve with rice.

NUTRITIONS:

1 serving: 368 calories, 14g fat (7g saturated fat), 84mg cholesterol, 1095mg sodium, 32g carbohydrate (28g sugars, 2g fiber), 28g protein.

ITALIAN SAUSAGE WITH PEPPERS AND ONION

PREP TIME
5 minutes
COOK TIME
27 minutes
TOTAL TIME
32 minutes

INGREDIENTS:

1 tablespoon oil
1 sweet pepper
1 small onion
4 Italian sausage links
4 sausage rolls, sliced down the middle

DIRECTIONS:

1:
Cut the sweet pepper into slices, removing the stem, seeds, and membranes.

2:
Cut the top and bottom of the onion and remove the outside layer. Cut the onion in half and cut both halves into long slices.

3:
Heat oil in an air fryer at 320 degrees for 1 minute in an air fryer sized pan.

4:
Add peppers and onions into the pan and cook on 320 for 10-12 minutes, stirring occasionally.

5:
Remove peppers and onions from air fryer.

6:
Increase air fryer temperature to 380 degrees and add Italian sausage links.

7:
Cook at 380 degrees for 10-12 minutes, moving basket halfway through to rotate.

8:
Remove Italian sausages from the air fryer.

9:
Assemble sausage links, peppers, and onions on the sausage rolls.

10:
Place back in the air fryer at 380 degrees and cook for 1-2 minutes to crisp up the sausage roll.

NUTRITIONS:

Amount Per Serving: CALORIES: 623 TOTAL FAT: 47g SATURATED FAT: 13g

AL PASTOR TACOS

PREP TIME
13 mins
COOK TIME
8 mins
TOTAL TIME
21 mins

INGREDIENTS:

2 lbs flap meat (flap steak or pork sirloin or any other cut of pork)
4 gloves fresh garlic, finely minced
2 tbsp dark brown sugar (I used Lakanto [monk fruit sweetener])
2 tsp kosher salt
1 ½ tsp ground cumin
1 ½ tsp dried oregano
1 ½ tsp ground achiote (annato seed [I used 1/2 tsp. ancho chile powder])
1 tsp chipotle peppers in adobo (I used just the sauce but you can chop up peppers too)
1 can pineapple rings in juice (or 1 fresh pineapple cut into rings)
10 fresh or prepared Paleo or Gluten Free tortillas
CONDIMENTS
homemade or packaged pico de gallo
1 fresh lime, cut into wedges
Avocado Cream (see recipe) or guacamole

DIRECTIONS:

1:
Freeze whatever meat you're using for at least 20 minutes to up to 4 hours. Or thaw until partially frozen. Slice thinly.

2
Slice pineapple into rings and core the center. Mince a small amount (about 1/4 cup) for marinating. Or use a can of pineapple slices or rings in juice.

3
Place meat in a medium bowl and add chipotle in adobo (or just sauce), oregano, cumin, achiote (or ancho chile powder), 1/4 cup pineapple juice (from canned pineapple) or minced pineapple, 1 Tbsp. brown sugar (or other sweetener), and salt. Cover and refrigerate for an hour or more.

4
Preheat air fryer to 400 degrees F for 5 minutes. Pull out air fryer drawer and lightly spray basket with cooking spray.

5
Place marinated meat in single layer in air fryer and cover with pineapple rings. sprinkle 1 Tbsp. brown sugar over pineapple.

6
Cook at 390 degrees F for 8 minutes. You may have to cook several batches.

7
Serve with warm tortillas, preferable grain-free, with pico de gallo, lime wedges, and Avocado Cream (recipe) or guacamole. Enjoy pineapple in taco or on the side.

EASY BBQ PORK SHREDDED PIZZA

Prep Time: 5 Cook Time: 10 Total Time: 15 Yield: 8 servings

INGREDIENTS:

1 package biscuit dough
1 cups shredded BBQ chicken or pork
1/2 cup shredded cheddar cheese

DIRECTIONS:

1
Start with rolling the biscuits out, with a rolling pin.
2
Transfer the rolled out dough, to your air fryer tray or basket. (either sprayed with olive oil)
3
Top with BBQ chicken or BBQ pork.
4
Sprinkle with grated cheese, and set into the air fryer for 6-9 minutes, at 330 degrees F.

EASY GREEK MEETBALLS

PREP TIME 10 mins
COOK TIME 10 mins

INGREDIENTS:

½ teaspoon garlic powder
½ teaspoon onion powder
½ teaspoon paprika
1½ teaspoons dried oregano
1 teaspoon dried mint (1.5 teaspoons semi-dried, or 7 to 8 leaves of fresh mint, finely chopped)
½ teaspoon salt
¼ teaspoon pepper
1 tablespoon olive oil
1 pound ground chicken UK/Australia = minced chicken – turkey, beef and pork also work
½ cup panko breadcrumbs or any breadcrumbs
1 egg
1 lemon zest only (then you can use the rest of the lemon for squeezing over at the end)

DIRECTIONS:

1
Line a baking tray with baking paper. Preheat the air fryer or oven to 400F/205C.

2
Put all of the Ingredients into a large bowl. Mix with a wooden spoon until well combined.

3
Shape the mixture into small bite-sized meatballs and place on the baking paper.

4
Air fry for 8 to 12 minutes until starting to go golden brown (basket-style air fryers tend to cook faster than oven-style air fryers). Cook in 2 batches if necessary. Turn or shake lightly half way through cooking. If baking, bake for 25 to 30 minutes, turning half way.

5
Serve with a Greek salad, tzatziki and bread, sweet potato wedges and vegetables, or turn into Greek wraps or tacos.

NUTRITIONS:

Calories: 168kcal
Carbohydrates: 6g
Protein: 15g

MEATBALL PARM SUB

COOK TIME
12 minutes
TOTAL TIME
12 minutes

INGREDIENTS:

2 tablespoons shredded Parmesan cheese
1/4 teaspoon dried oregano
8 frozen meatballs
2 sub or sausage rolls
1 cup marinara sauce (room temperature or warmed)

DIRECTIONS:

1
Preheat air fryer to 320 degrees.

2
Cook the frozen meatballs for 9-11 minutes shaking halfway through until the internal temperature reaches 160 degrees.

3
Remove the meatballs from the air fryer and toss in the marinara sauce and oregano.

4
Add meatballs to sub rolls and spoon on 2 tablespoons of marinara sauce on top remaining from the bowl.

5
Top sub sandwich with freshly grated Parmesan cheese.

6
Turn air fryer to 350 degrees, slowly place meatball parm subs inside the air fryer and cook for 2 minutes until the cheese is melted and sauce is warmed.

7
Carefully remove subs from the air fryer, top with more Parmesan cheese if desired and enjoy!

CHAPTER 2:

POULTRY

RECIPES

CHICKEN FAJITA TAQUITOS

Prep:
20 mins
Cook:
25 mins
Additional:
2 hrs
Total:
2 hrs 45 mins
Servings:
24
Yield:
24 taquitos

INGREDIENTS:

1 pound corn tortillas
1 (14 ounce) package fire-roasted peppers and onion blend, thawed
1 cup shredded Mexican cheese blend
cooking spray
2 (4 ounce) boneless, skinless chicken breasts, cut into strips
1 ¼ cups mojo criollo marinade

DIRECTIONS:

1
Place chicken strips in a sealable container and add marinade. Seal and allow to marinate for 2 hours.

2
Drain off marinade and discard. Heat a skillet over medium-high heat and cook chicken strips until browned, 6 to 7 minutes. Add thawed peppers and onions and cook for 2 to 3 minutes more.

3
Transfer chicken strips to a cutting board and chop into smaller pieces. Add chopped chicken back to the peppers and onions; stir to combine.

4
Preheat an heat air fryer to 370 degrees F (187 degrees C) for 5 minutes.

5
Place tortillas in a tortilla bag. Microwave 5 tortillas at a time for 30 seconds.

6
Spray each side of warmed tortillas with about 1/2 teaspoon oil and lay on a cutting board. Place 1 to 2 tablespoons chicken filling on top and sprinkle with 1 tablespoon cheese blend. Roll taquitos up tightly.

7
Place taquitos seam-side down in the air fryer basket and air fry for 5 minutes. Increase air fryer temperature to 400 degrees F (200 degrees C) and air fry for 5 minutes more.

NUTRITIONS:

Per Serving: 78 calories; protein 4.5g; carbohydrates 9.6g; fat 2.6g

CHICKEN NUGGETS

Prep:
15 mins
Cook:
15 mins
Total:
30 mins
Servings:
8
Yield:
8 servings

INGREDIENTS:

1 tablespoon paprika
1 tablespoon parsley flakes
1 teaspoon salt
1 teaspoon ground black pepper
2 eggs
2 cups panko bread crumbs
cooking spray
1 cup buttermilk
2 pounds chicken tenderloins, cut into nugget size
1 cup flour
3 tablespoons grated Parmesan cheese

DIRECTIONS:

1

Mix buttermilk and chicken in a large bowl and let soak while you prepare the seasoned flour.

2

Combine flour, Parmesan cheese, paprika, parsley, salt, and pepper in a large bowl. Beat eggs in a separate bowl. Pour bread crumbs onto a flat plate.

3

Dredge each chicken nugget first in flour, then in beaten egg, and finally coat in breadcrumbs.

4

Preheat the air fryer to 400 degrees F (200 degrees C). Spray the basket with cooking spray. Place as many nuggets into the basket as you can without overcrowding. Lightly mist the tops of the nuggets with cooking spray.

5

Cook for 10 minutes. Flip chicken nuggets and cook for an additional 2 minutes. Remove and repeat with remaining nuggets.

NUTRITIONS:

310 calories; protein 33.4g; carbohydrates 33.5g; fat 6.8g

MARINATED CHICKEN BREASTS

INGREDIENTS:

Chicken:

4 8 oz boneless, skinless chicken breasts
Olive oil cooking spray

Chicken Marinade:

¼ cup olive oil
¼ cup freshly squeezed lemon juice
3 tbsp Worcestershire Sauce
3 medium cloves garlic minced
½ tsp salt
½ tsp black pepper
2 tbsp fresh oregano minced or 2 teaspoons dried oregano
¼ cup fresh parsley minced and lightly packed or 4 teaspoons dried parsley
¼ cup fresh basil minced and lightly packed or 4 teaspoons dried basil

DIRECTIONS:

1
In a large bowl, whisk together Ingredients for the marinade. Add chicken breast to a large container or resealable bag, pour marinade over chicken, seal or cover.

2
Chill in the refrigerator for up to 4 hours.

3
Remove from the refrigerator and let your chicken reach room temperature. (20-30 minutes)

4
Preheat your air fryer to 370° F for 5 minutes.

5
Remove the air fryer basket and place chicken breasts inside, leaving room between the breasts, so they cook evenly.

6
Spray each chicken breast with olive oil.

7
Place back into preheated air fryer and cook for 10 minutes

8
Remove the basket and flip breasts over, spray again with olive oil and cook for another 6-8 minutes; chicken is done when the internal temperature reaches 160° F when checked with an instant-read thermometer.

9
Remove your chicken from the air fryer basket and allow it to rest for 5 minutes before serving!

10
Garnish chicken with fresh oregano, parsley, and/or basil.

NUTRITIONS:

Calories: 274kcal | Carbohydrates: 5g | Protein: 25g | Fat: 17g | Saturated Fat: 3g

HEALTHY BREAKFAST FRITTATA

Prep:
15 mins
Cook:
20 mins
Total:
35 mins
Servings:
2
Yield:
2 servings

INGREDIENTS:

1 green onion, chopped
1 pinch cayenne pepper (Optional)
cooking spray
¼ pound breakfast sausage, fully cooked and crumbled
4 eggs, lightly beaten
½ cup shredded Cheddar-Monterey Jack cheese blend
2 tablespoons red bell pepper, diced

DIRECTIONS:

1

Combine sausage, eggs, Cheddar-Monterey Jack cheese, bell pepper, onion, and cayenne in a bowl and mix to combine.

2

Preheat the air fryer to 360 degrees F (180 degrees C). Spray a nonstick 6x2-inch cake pan with cooking spray.

3

Place egg mixture in the prepared cake pan.

4

Cook in the air fryer until frittata is set, 18 to 20 minutes.

NUTRITIONS:

380 calories; protein 31.2g; carbohydrates 2.9g; fat 27.4g

GLUTEN FREE CHICKEN

Prep Time
10 mins
Cook Time
20 mins
Total Time
30 mins

INGREDIENTS:

½ teaspoon salt
¼ teaspoon freshly ground black pepper
¼ cup gluten-free all purpose flour
1 large egg, lightly beaten
2 large (approximately 10-ounce) chicken breasts, boneless, skinless
olive oil cooking spray
½ cup corn meal
2 tablspoons fresh lemon zest
2 teaspoons fresh thyme, finely chopped
¾ teaspoon garlic powder
¾ teaspoon smoked paprika

DIRECTIONS:

1
Add the corn meal, lemon zest, thyme, garlic powder, paprika, salt and pepper to a large, shallow bowl. Mix to blend evenly and set aside.

2
Add the flour to a second large, shallow bowl, and the egg to a third.

3
Sprinkle the chicken breasts lightly with salt and pepper, and one at a time, coat them with the flour lightly and evenly. Then dip them into the egg, being sure they're well coated. Now place each breast on top of the corn meal mixture and gently press down so that it adheres to it, and do the same thing on the other side, and edges.

4
Remove the basket from the pot of the air fryer, and line the pot with foil. Return the basket and spray the bottom of it with the olive oil.
Place the coated chicken breasts in the basket and then spray the top surface with the olive oil.

5
For the GoWISE USA Air Fryer, use the Preset Chicken setting for 20 minutes at 400° F.

6
Let the air fryer cool down and wait for the indicator that it's ready to open.

GARLIC PARMESAN CHICKEN TENDER

PREP TIME
5 mins
COOK TIME
12 mins

INGREDIENTS:

8 chicken tenders, raw
1 egg
2 tablespoons of water
canola or non-fat cooking spray
For the dredge coating:
1 cup panko breadcrumbs
1/2 tsp salt
1/4 tsp ground black pepper, more or less to taste
1 tsp garlic powder
1/2 tsp onion powder
1/4 cup parmesan cheese
Pictured here served with Homemade Ranch Dressing.

DIRECTIONS:

1
Combine the dredge coating Ingredients in a shallow bowl or baking pan large enough to fit the chicken pieces.

2
In a second shallow bowl or baking pan, place egg and water and whisk to combine.

3
Dip chicken tenders into the egg wash and then into the panko dredge mixture.

4
Place the breaded tenders into the fry basket. Repeat with remaining tenders.

5
Spray a light coat of canola oil or non-fat cooking spray over the panko.

6
Set the temperature to 400 degrees and fry for 12 minutes. Check the chicken halfway through the cooking time and turn the chicken over to brown the other side.

7
Note: The cooking time may be more or less depending on the size and thickness of your chicken tenders, finers or nuggets, and the quantity of chicken in the basket.

NUTRITIONS:

Calories: 220kcal
Carbohydrates: 13g
Protein: 27g

EASY CHICKEN MANCHURIAN

Prep time
5 mins
Cook time
15 mins
Total time
20 mins

INGREDIENTS:

Chicken pieces, boneless - 250 grams.
Salt - to taste.
Pepper powder - 1/2 tea spoon.
Egg - 1 numbers.
All purpose flour - 1 tablespoon.
Corn starch - 1 tablespoon.
Onion(chopped) - 1 number.
Green chillies(chopped) - 2 numbers.
Msg - 1 pinch.
Soya sauce - 1 tea spoon.
Chili paste - 1/2 tea spoon.
Sugar - 1 pinch.
Water - 1/2 cup.
Spring onions(chopped) - 1 tablespoon.
Cashew nuts - 8 numbers.
Garlic(chopped) - 1/2 tea spoon.
Ginger(chopped) - 1/2 tea spoon.

DIRECTIONS:

1

In a bowl, put in the chicken pieces, add a little salt, pinch of pepper, little egg and mix well.

2

In a plate, put all-purpose, corn starch, mix well and add the chicken pieces and coat well. Brush very little oil the chicken pieces.

3

Preheat the air fryer and then put the chicken pieces into the air fryer at 180 degrees C for 7-8 minutes and fry them until done.

4

In a pan, add very little oil, few cashew nuts, and apinch of salt to color them.

5

Add finely chopped garlic, ginger, and salt. Add chopped onions and fry till they are translucent.

6

Add a little salt, green chilies, pepper powder, MSG, soya sauce, chili paste, little water, and mix. Add a pinch of sugar and mix again.

7

Add in the air fried chicken pieces and toss well.

8

Garnish with some spring onions and serve hot.

BARBECUE CHICKEN

READY IN:
36min
PREP TIME:
15min
COOK TIME:
21min

INGREDIENTS:

1 whole (4 pound) chicken, cut into thigh, leg, and breast pieces
1 1/4 teaspoons salt
1 1/4 teaspoons smoked paprika
1 1/4 teaspoons garlic powder
1 1/4 cups barbeque sauce

DIRECTIONS:

1
Preheat air fryer to 375°F (190°C).

2
Coat chicken pieces in salt, paprika, and garlic powder and place skin-side down in air fryer basket, working in batches as needed.

3
Cook chicken in the air fryer until golden brown, about 18 minutes. Transfer chicken to a plate and brush all over with BBQ sauce.

4
Wipe chicken fat out of air fryer basket to prevent excess smoking.

5
Return chicken to air fryer basket, skin-side up, and cook at 350°F (180°C) until a meat thermometer inserted into the thickest part of a thigh reads 165°F (75°C), about 3 minutes.

6
Serve immediately with additional BBQ sauce.

CHAPTER 3: MEAT RECIPES

STEAK WITH GARLIC HERB AND BUTTER

Prep Time 20 minutes
Cook Time 12 minutes
Resting Time 5 minutes
Total Time 32 minutes

INGREDIENTS:

2 8 oz Ribeye steak
salt
freshly cracked black pepper
olive oil
Garlic Butter
1 stick unsalted butter softened
2 Tbsp fresh parsley chopped
2 tsp garlic minced
1 tsp Worcestershire Sauce
1/2 tsp salt

DIRECTIONS:

1
Prepare Garlic Butter by mixing butter, parsley garlic, worcestershire sauce, and salt until thoroughly combined.

2
Place in parchment paper and roll into a log. Refrigerate until ready to use.

3
Remove steak from fridge and allow to sit at room temperature for 20 minutes. Rub a little bit of olive oil on both side of the steak and season with salt and freshly cracked black pepper.

4
Grease your Air Fryer basket by rubbing a little bit of oil on the basket. Preheat Air Fryer to 400 degrees Fahrenheit. Once preheated, place steaks in air fryer and cook for 12 minutes, flipping halfway through.*

5
Remove from air fryer and allow to rest for 5 minutes. Top with garlic butter.

NUTRITIONS:

Calories: 683kcal

NEW YORK STRIP STEAK

PREP TIME
5 minutes
COOK TIME
15 minutes
ADDITIONAL TIME
30 minutes
TOTAL TIME
50 minutes

INGREDIENTS:

2-3 cloves garlic, minced finely or zested
1 tablespoon Parsley, minced fine (dried or fresh is fine)
1/2 teaspoon salt
1/2 teaspoon pepper
1 New York, boneless 1 1/4" in thickness (12-16 ounces)
1 teaspoon Olive Oil
Salt and pepper to season (generously)
2 tablespoons Salted Butter, softened

DIRECTIONS:

1
Let ribeye steak sit on the counter for 30 minutes before cooking.

2
While the steak is coming to room temperature you'll want to make the garlic butter. To softened butter add garlic, salt, pepper and parsley and mix well. You can roll into a log and place in the freezer to help make it more solid or you can leave it on a bowl and place it into the fridge to set while the steak cooks.

3
Preheat your air fryer to 390- 400° (whichever your Air Fryer is able to go to for 7 minutes.

4
While the air fryer is heating, brush the steak with olive oil then season your steak with salt and pepper generously on both sides

5
Once the air fryer has been preheated you'll place the steak into the air fryer. If you have a rack, you'll want to place the steak onto the rack. If no rack is available place the steak on the bottom.

6
Cook for 7 minutes, then open the air fryer and quickly flip the steak. Cook for an additional 7 minutes for Medium rare. If you want rare you'll cook a minute less each side, and if you want well done, you'll cook for 1-2 minutes more each side.

7
Once your steak has achieved your desired doneness. you'll want to remove it from the air fryer and place it on a cutting board to rest for 5-10 minutes.

8
Cut a couple of slices of the butter and place them on top of the steak while it rests.

9
Slice at an angle about 1/2- 1" thick. Serve on a serving plate with additional dollops of butter on top for people to serve themselves.

NUTRITIONS:

CALORIES: 246 TOTAL FAT: 22g saturated FAT: 11g trans FAT: 0g unsaturated FAT: 10g

MOROCCAN MEATBALLS

prep time: 10 MINUTES
cook time: 40 MINUTES
total time: 50 MINUTES

INGREDIENTS:

1/2 Tbsp Zaatar
1 Egg
30 g (1 oz) Breadcrumbs
1/2 Tsp Salt
50 ml (1.75 fl oz) Pomegranate Molasses
Oil spray or olive oil for cooking.
200 g (7 oz) Minced Beef
75 g (2.75 oz) Onion
50 g (1.75 oz) Dried Apricots
25 g (0.75 oz) Nibbed almonds
1 Tbsp Harissa Paste

DIRECTIONS:

1 Dice the onion as finely as you can and add it to a bowl with the minced beef.
2 Cut the dried apricots into a small 3mm dice and add it to the bowl.
3 Add the almonds, zaatar and egg and mix well together.
4 Using wet hands form into 10 meatballs, they should be around 45g each (1.5 oz).

VENISON BURGERS

Prep:
5 mins
Cook:
16 mins
Total:
21 mins
Servings:
4
Yield:
4 burgers

INGREDIENTS:

½ teaspoon onion powder
½ teaspoon ground black pepper
4 hamburger buns
1 pound ground venison
2 teaspoons Worcestershire sauce
1 teaspoon seasoned salt

DIRECTIONS:

1
Preheat the air fryer to 400 degrees F (200 degrees C) according to manufacturer's instructions.

2
Combine venison, Worcestershire sauce, seasoned salt, onion powder, and ground pepper in a large bowl. Mix with your hands until evenly combined. Form mixture into 4 patties.

3
Place 2 patties in the basket of the air fryer and cook for 6 minutes. Carefully flip the patties and cook for 2 minutes more. Transfer to a paper towel-lined plate and repeat with remaining patties.

4
Serve on hamburger buns with your favorite condiments and toppings.

NUTRITIONS:

247 calories; protein 27.2g; carbohydrates 22.5g; fat 4.5g

TACO STUFFED AVOCADOS

PREP TIME
15 mins
COOK TIME
10 mins
TOTAL TIME
25 mins

INGREDIENTS:

1/2 cup cojack cheese small dice
1/2 cup cherry tomatoes halved
1/3 cup tortilla chips crushed
1/2 cup sour cream
4 avocados
1 lb hamburger
1 bunch scallions sliced
1 packet taco seasoning
1/4 cup water

DIRECTIONS:

1

In a large skillet, brown ground beef and scallions breaking it up with a wooden spoon, and cook until b rowned and cooked through, 8 minutes.

2

Stir in taco seasoning and water. Stir until sauce forms and thickens.

3

Slice avocados in half and remove seed.

4

Peel avocados. When you're holding the avocado half – you can use your knife to score the avocado on one end. The skin should peel right off like an orange. Just be gentle so you're not squeezing the avocado.

5

Scoop out a little extra from the pit area to make a nice round space in each avocado

6

Dip base of avocado half in sour cream and then in crushed tortilla chips

7

Place avocado halves, chip side down, in air fryer

8

Spoon taco meat into each avocado half

9

Take 2-3 small diced pieces of cheese and push them down into the taco meat.

10

Top with remaining crushed chips

11

Air fry at 350 for 10 minutes

12

Remove avocados from air fryer and serve with sides of sour cream, tomatoes and green onions

STEAK AND CHEESE SANDWICH

INGREDIENTS:

1 medium onion, sliced into half moons
2 small bell peppers, sliced into strips
Salt & fresh cracked black pepper (to taste)
1 pound rib-eye steak, shaved or cut into thin strips
Montreal Steak Seasoning (or your favorite, to taste)
Olive oil spray
4 – 6 slices provolone cheese
2 Italian sub rolls
Butter (to taste)

DIRECTIONS:

1 In a small bowl, add the sliced onions and bell peppers.
2 Spritz with olive oil spray to coat. Season with salt and fresh ground black pepper.
3 In the basket of your air fryer, add the onion and bell pepper slices.
4 Cook at 370 degrees for approximately 8 – 10 minutes.
5 When the onions and bell peppers are done, remove to a small bowl. Set aside.
6 Spritz the steak with olive oil spray to coat. Season with Montreal Steak Seasoning (or your favorite) to your taste.
7 Add the steak to the air fryer basket.
8 Cook at 380 degrees for approximately 2 – 3 minutes. Remove basket and flip. Return the basket to the air fryer for about 1 additional minute (or cook to your desired doneness).
9 Remove the steak from the air fryer. Set aside.
10 Split the sub roll and butter each side.
11 Put the roll into the air fryer inside facing up.

12 Top with steak, onions, bell peppers, and cheese.
13 Toast and melt the cheese in the air fryer at 350 degrees for approximately 2 - 3 minutes.
14 Remove the sandwich from the air fryer.
15 Fold to close and cut in half.
16 Plate with chips, fries, or salad.

BEEF WONTONS

Prep:
20 mins
Cook:
10 mins
Total:
30 mins
Servings:
24
Yield:
24 wontons

INGREDIENTS:

¼ teaspoon ground black pepper
¼ teaspoon ground ginger
½ (16 ounce) package 4 1/2-inch wonton wrappers
2 tablespoons sesame oil
1 pound lean ground beef
2 tablespoons finely chopped green onions
½ teaspoon salt
½ teaspoon garlic powder

DIRECTIONS:

1
Combine ground beef, green onions, salt, garlic powder, pepper, and ginger in a bowl; mix well.

2
Preheat the air fryer to 350 degrees F (175 degrees C).

3
Place several of the wonton wrappers on a plate or a cutting board without overlapping. Pour some water into a small bowl next to the plate.

4
Form about 1 tablespoon of beef mixture into a ball and place on one side of each wrapper. Dip your fingertips in the bowl of water and swipe some water around the edges of the wonton wrappers. Fold the wontons in half so that they form a triangle around the beef mixture. Wet your fingers with additional water and pinch the edges of the wrapper together. Place folded wontons onto plates, making sure they don't overlap, while you assemble the remaining wontons.

5
Brush one side of the wontons lightly with sesame oil. Place a single layer of wontons into the air fryer basket, oiled side down. Brush the tops lightly with additional sesame oil.

6
Air fry for 4 minutes, then carefully flip the wontons with tongs. Cook on the second side until the wontons are crispy and the edges are golden brown, 3 to 4 more minutes. Transfer wontons to a paper towel-lined plate and let cool while you cook the rest of the wontons in batches.

NUTRITIONS:

74 calories; protein 4.6g; carbohydrates 5.5g; fat 3.6g

CHAPTER 4:

VEGETABLE

RECIPES

ZUCCHINI CURLY FRIES

Prep:
15 mins
Cook:
20 mins
Total:
35 mins
Servings:
4
Yield:
4 servings

INGREDIENTS:

1 cup panko bread crumbs
½ cup grated Parmesan cheese
1 teaspoon Italian seasoning
nonstick cooking spray
1 zucchini
1 egg, beaten

DIRECTIONS:

1
Preheat an air fryer to 400 degrees F (200 degrees C).

2
Cut zucchini into spirals using a spiralizer fitted with the large shredding blade.

3
Place egg in a shallow dish. Combine bread crumbs, Parmesan cheese, and Italian seasoning in a large resealable plastic bag. Dip 1/2 of the spiralized zucchini in the beaten egg and then place in the bag to coat with bread crumb mixture.

4
Spray the basket of the air fryer with cooking spray. Arrange breaded zucchini fries in the prepared basket, making sure to not overcrowd. Spray the tops with cooking spray.

5
Cook until crispy, about 10 minutes, flipping halfway through cook time. Transfer fries to a paper towel-lined plate. Repeat breading and cooking process with remaining zucchini spirals.

NUTRITIONS:

136 calories; protein 8.6g; carbohydrates 20.5g; fat 5.1g

EASY ROASTED ASPARAGUS

Prep:
10 mins
Cook:
10 mins
Total:
20 mins
Servings:
2
Yield:
2 servings

INGREDIENTS:

½ teaspoon Himalayan pink salt
¼ teaspoon ground multi-colored peppercorns
¼ teaspoon red pepper flakes
¼ cup freshly grated Parmesan cheese
1 bunch fresh asparagus, trimmed
avocado oil cooking spray
½ teaspoon garlic powder

DIRECTIONS:

1

Preheat the air fryer to 375 degrees F (190 degrees C). Line the basket with parchment paper.

2

Place asparagus spears in the air fryer basket and mist with avocado oil. Sprinkle with garlic powder, pink Himalayan salt, pepper, and red pepper flakes. Top with Parmesan cheese.

3

Air fry until asparagus spears start to char, 7 to 9 minutes.

NUTRITIONS:

94 calories; protein 9g; carbohydrates 10.1g; fat 3.3g

STUFFED MUSHROOMS

Prep:
20 mins
Cook:
10 mins
Additional:
5 mins
Total:
35 mins
Servings:
6
Yield:
6 servings

INGREDIENTS:

¼ cup finely shredded sharp Cheddar cheese
¼ teaspoon ground paprika
1 pinch salt
cooking spray
1 (16 ounce) package whole white button mushrooms
2 scallions
4 ounces cream cheese, softened

DIRECTIONS:

1
Using a damp cloth, gently clean mushrooms. Remove stems and discard.

2
Mince scallions and separate white and green parts.

3
Preheat an air fryer to 360 degrees F (182 degrees C).

4
Combine cream cheese, Cheddar cheese, the white parts from the scallions, paprika, and salt in a small bowl. Stuff filling into the mushrooms, pressing it in to fill the cavity with the back of a small spoon.

5
Spray the air fryer basket with cooking spray and set mushrooms inside. Depending on the size of your air fryer, you may have to do 2 batches.

6
Cook mushrooms until filling is lightly browned, about 8 minutes. Repeat with remaining mushrooms.

7
Sprinkle mushrooms with scallion greens and let cool for 5 minutes before serving.

NUTRITIONS:

104 calories; protein 5g; carbohydrates 3.5g; fat 8.4g

ITALIAN RATATOUILLE

Prep:
25 mins
Cook:
25 mins
Additional:
5 mins
Total:
55 mins

INGREDIENTS:

5 sprigs fresh basil, stemmed and chopped
2 sprigs fresh oregano, stemmed and chopped
1 clove garlic, crushed
salt and ground black pepper to taste
1 tablespoon olive oil
1 tablespoon white wine
1 teaspoon vinegar
½ small eggplant, cut into cubes
1 zucchini, cut into cubes
1 medium tomato, cut into cubes
½ large yellow bell pepper, cut into cubes
½ large red bell pepper, cut into cubes
½ onion, cut into cubes
1 fresh cayenne pepper, diced

DIRECTIONS:

1

Preheat an air fryer to 400 degrees F (200 degrees C).

2

Place eggplant, zucchini, tomato, bell peppers, and onion in a bowl. Add cayenne pepper, basil, oregano, garlic, salt, and pepper. Mix well to distribute everything evenly. Drizzle in oil, wine, and vinegar, mixing to coat all the vegetables.

3

Pour vegetable mixture into a baking dish and insert into the basket of the air fryer. Cook for 8 minutes. Stir; cook for another 8 minutes. Stir again and continue cooking until tender, stirring every 5 minutes, 10 to 15 minutes more. Turn off air fryer, leaving dish inside. Let rest for 5 minutes before serving.

NUTRITIONS:

79 calories; protein 2.1g; carbohydrates 10.2g; fat 3.8g

ZUCCHINI FRITTERS

prep time: 5 MINUTES cook time: 15 MINUTES total time: 20 MINUTES

INGREDIENTS:

1 egg
1/2 cup flour
2 tbs chives
1 tsp salt
1 tsp pepper
2 Zucchini's
1 cup shredded cheddar

DIRECTIONS:

1 Shred Zucchinis and squeeze out excess water with a cheesecloth
2 Add zucchini, egg, flour, chives, salt, and pepper to a bowl.
3 Mix together.
4 Make 8 patties with the mixture
5 Optional (place in the freezer for 5-10 minutes) to keep the form
6 Place air fryer on 350
7 Put zucchini patties in the air fryer for 5 minutes
8 Flip over the pattie for an additional 5-10 minutes or until brown

NUTRITIONS:

CALORIES: 104 TOTAL FAT: 6g SATURATED FAT: 3g TRANS FAT: 0g UNSATURATED FAT: 2g

CRISPY GNOCCHI

Prep Time
5 mins
Cook Time
13 mins
Total Time
18 mins

INGREDIENTS:

1 lb gnocchi 450 g; see note 1
1 tablespoon olive oil
½ teaspoon salt
½ teaspoon garlic powder

DIRECTIONS:

1 Heat air fryer to 200°C/390°F.
2 Toss gnocchi with olive oil, salt and garlic powder until evenly coated.
3 Transfer gnocchi to the air fryer basket.
4 Cook for a total time of 13 minutes, shaking 3-4 times during the cooking process. Gnocchi should be golden and crispy

NUTRITIONS:

Calories: 216kcal | Carbohydrates: 40g | Protein: 5g | Fat: 4g

CARROTS WITH TAHINI-LEMON SAUCE

Prep:
10 mins
Cook:
10 mins
Total:
20 mins
Servings:
2
Yield:
2 servings

INGREDIENTS:

1 tablespoon tahini
1 tablespoon lemon juice
1 pinch garlic powder
1 pinch cayenne pepper
1 tablespoon chopped fresh parsley
1 pinch Aleppo pepper (Optional)
3 large carrots, peeled and cut into sticks
1 tablespoon grapeseed oil
¼ teaspoon ground cumin
¼ teaspoon ground coriander
1 pinch salt and ground black pepper to taste
1 ½ tablespoons plain yogurt

DIRECTIONS:

1
Preheat the air fryer to 390 degrees F (200 degrees C).

2
Toss carrot sticks with oil, cumin, coriander, salt, and pepper in a large bowl. Transfer to the air fryer basket and set timer for 5 minutes. Shake the basket and continue cooking until carrots are tender and starting to brown, about 5 minutes more.

3
Meanwhile, whisk yogurt, tahini, lemon juice, garlic, and cayenne in a small bowl. Season with salt.

4
Plate carrots and drizzle the sauce on top. Garnish with parsley and aleppo flakes.

NUTRITIONS:

164 calories; protein 3.2g; carbohydrates 14.4g

MEDITERRANEAN VEGETABLES MEDLEY

Prep:
10 mins
Cook:
20 mins
Total:
30 mins
Servings:
4
Yield:
3 1/2 cups

INGREDIENTS:

1 cup shiitake mushrooms, stemmed and sliced
1 cup grape tomatoes
2 tablespoons olive oil
2 cloves garlic, minced
½ teaspoon dried oregano
½ teaspoon kosher salt
1 teaspoon lemon zest
½ small eggplant, cut into 1/4-inch slices
1 small zucchini, cut into 1/4-inch slices
1 small summer squash, cut into 1/4-inch slices

DIRECTIONS:

1

Preheat the oven to 200 degrees F (95 degrees C).

2

Cut eggplant slices into wedges and place in a large bowl. Add zucchini, summer squash, mushrooms, tomatoes, olive oil, garlic, oregano, and salt; toss to combine. Place vegetables in a single layer in the air fryer basket, working in small batches if necessary.

3

Cook vegetables in the air fryer at 360 degrees F (182 degrees C) for 5 minutes. Stir, and continue to cook until tender and edges turn golden brown, about 5 minutes more. Transfer vegetables to a baking pan and place in the preheated oven to keep warm while cooking remaining vegetables.

4

Sprinkle vegetables with lemon zest before serving.

NUTRITIONS:

105 calories; protein 2.4g; carbohydrates 8.9g

GRILLED VEGGIES AND COUS COUS

PREP TIME
10 minutes
COOK TIME
8 minutes
TOTAL TIME
18 minutes

INGREDIENTS:

¾ zucchini
1 paprika
125 g mushrooms
200 g shrimp
2 tsp Italian herbs
150 g couscous
150 ml water
2 tbsp herb cheese

DIRECTIONS:

1
Cut the zucchini, paprika and mushrooms into cubes and put them in a bowl.

2 Add the Italian herbs and add salt and pepper to taste. Then shake well, so that all vegetables are seasoned.

3
Put a pan with 150 ml water on the stove and add a little bit of salt.

4
Bake the vegetables in the basket of your Air Fryer for 8 minutes at 180 °C. Add the shrimps after 2 minutes. The vegetables will still be a bit crispy after 8 minutes, so if you like them a bit softer, you can make it 10 minutes (and add the shrimps after 4 minutes).

5
When the water boils, take the pan off the pit and add your couscous. Use a fork to stir a bit until it has soaked up all the water (that takes about 2 minutes). Leave it in the pan. Shake the vegetables and shrimp several times for best results.

6
Take them out, put them back in the bowl add the herb cheese to finish up and serve

CHAPTER 5:

FISH & SEAFOOD RECIPES

COCONUT PRAWNS

MAKES:
4 SERVINGS
PREP TIME:
5 MINS
TOTAL TIME:
30 MINS

INGREDIENTS:

For The Prawns:

65 g plain flour
Salt
Freshly ground black pepper
100 g panko bread crumbs
35 g shredded sweetened coconut
2 large eggs, beaten
450 g large prawns, peeled and deveined, tails on

For The Dipping Sauce:

120 g mayonnaise
1 tbsp. Sriracha
1 tbsp. Thai sweet chilli saucE

DIRECTIONS:

1 In a shallow bowl, season flour with salt and pepper. In another shallow bowl, combine bread crumbs and coconut. Place eggs in a third shallow bowl.

2 Working with one at a time, dip prawns in flour, then eggs, then coconut mixture.

3 Place prawns in the basket of an air fryer and heat to 200°C. Bake until prawns are golden and cooked through, 10 to 12 minutes. Work in batches as necessary.

4 In a small bowl, combine mayonnaise, Sriracha, and chilli sauce. Serve prawns with dipping sauce.

CAJUN SALMON

Prep:
10 mins
Cook:
10 mins
Total:
20 mins
Servings:
2
Yield:
2 servings

INGREDIENTS:

2 (6 ounce) skin-on salmon fillets
cooking spray
1 tablespoon Cajun seasoning
1 teaspoon brown sugar

DIRECTIONS:

1

Preheat the air fryer to 390 degrees F (200 degrees C).

2

Rinse and dry salmon fillets with a paper towel. Mist fillets with cooking spray. Combine Cajun seasoning and brown sugar in a small bowl. Sprinkle onto a plate. Press flesh sides of fillets into the seasoning mixture.

3

Spray the basket of the air fryer with cooking spray and place salmon fillets skin-side down. Mist salmon again lightly with cooking spray.

4

Cook for 8 minutes. Remove from air fryer and let rest for 2 minutes before serving.

NUTRITIONS:

327 calories; protein 33.7g; carbohydrates 4g

HEALTHY AND TASTY FISHCAKES

Prep Time:
15 minutes
Cook Time:
15 minutes
Chill time before cooking:
30 minutes
Total Time:
1 hour

INGREDIENTS:

10 ounces mashed potatoes
10 ounces imitation crab meat (or fish of your choice)
1 egg
salt and pepper (to taste)
1 tbsp grainy mustard
1 tbsp chopped green onion
1/2 cup bread crumbs (for coating)
cooking spray

DIRECTIONS:

To Make the Fish Cakes:

1. Take about 2 large potatoes. Peel, cut and boil until tender. Once cooked, drain and mash (enough to make 10 ounces). Set aside.
2. In a food processor combine the fish, salt, pepper, and egg. Pulse 3-4 times until smooth.
3. Place the fish mixture, mashed potatoes, mustard and green onion in a large bowl. Combine with a rubber spatula.
4. Place the breadcrumbs in a shallow dish (with a rim).
5. Divide the fish mixture into 6 portions.
6. Form each portion into a patty. (Roll into a ball, and lightly press to form a thick patty).
7. Coat each patty on all sides with the breadcrumbs.
8. Place the patties on a plate, cover with plastic wrap and place in the fridge for at least 30 minutes to chill.

To Cook the Fish Cakes:

1. Turn your air fryer on to 425º F.
2. Remove the fish cakes from the fridge.
3. Place them in the cooking basket of your air fryer. Depending on your model, you may have to cook these in 2 batches if they don't all fit in the basket.
4. Spray them lightly with cooking spray on both sides.
5. Place in the air fryer and cook for 10-15 minutes (or until golden brown). I turned the patties over around the 1/2 way mark.

FISH STICKS

Prep:
10 mins
Cook:
10 mins
Total:
20 mins
Servings:
4
Yield:
4 servings

INGREDIENTS:

½ cup panko bread crumbs
¼ cup grated Parmesan cheese
1 tablespoon parsley flakes
1 teaspoon paprika
½ teaspoon black pepper
cooking spray
1 pound cod fillets
¼ cup all-purpose flour
1 egg

DIRECTIONS:

1

Preheat an air fryer to 400 degrees F (200 degrees C).

2

Pat fish dry with paper towels and cut into 1x3-inch sticks.

3

Place flour in a shallow dish. Beat egg in a separate shallow dish. Combine panko, Parmesan cheese, parsley, paprika, and pepper in a third shallow dish.

4

Coat each fish stick in flour, then dip in beaten egg, and finally coat in seasoned panko mixture.

5

Spray the basket of the air fryer with nonstick cooking spray. Arrange 1/2 the sticks in the basket, making sure none are touching. Spray the top of each stick with cooking spray.

6

Cook in the preheated air fryer for 5 minutes. Flip fish sticks and cook an additional 5 minutes. Repeat with remaining fish sticks

NUTRITIONS:

200 calories; protein 26.3g; carbohydrates 16.5g;

EASY BREADED SHRIMP

Prep Time: 15 minutes Cook Time: 6 minutes Total Time: 21 minutes

INGREDIENTS:

1 lb shrimp shelled, cleaned and deveined
1/4 cup flour
1/2 tsp salt
1 egg
1/2 cup panko bread crumbs

DIRECTIONS:

1 Clean and dry shrimp.
2 You need three shallow bowls. Add flour and salt to one bowl, egg to another bowl, and breadcrumbs to the third bowl. Start by coating the shrimp in flour, then dip it in the egg mixture, then coat it with breadcrumbs. Bread all the shrimp this way.
3 Preheat the air fryer to 400 degrees F.
4 Lightly spray air fryer basket with oil and place shrimp in the basket leaving space between each shrimp. Lightly spray the tops of the shrimp.
5 Cook for 3 minutes. Flip shrimp over and cook an additional 3 minutes. Cook for 4 minutes per side for larger shrimp. Continue in small batches until all shrimp are cooked.

NUTRITIONS:

Calories: 187kcal | Carbohydrates: 11g | Protein: 26g | Fat: 3g | Saturated Fat: 1g | Cholesterol: 327mg | Sodium: 1242mg

SHRIMP SANDWICH WITH TARTAR SAUCE

PREP TIME:
10 mins
COOK TIME:
20 mins
TOTAL TIME:
30 mins

INGREDIENTS:

20 about 14 to 16 oz raw peeled and deveined jumbo shrimp, tails removed
1 large egg beaten
1/3 cup dry seasoned panko crumbs
1/2 cup whole wheat seasoned breadcrumbs
olive oil spray
1 head butter lettuce, leaves separated
4 whole wheat 100 calorie potato buns, (round or long) I like Martins
Tartar Sauce:
1/4 cup reduced fat sour cream
3 tablespoons light mayonnaise
1/3 cup finely chopped dill pickles
1 tablespoon fresh chopped dill
1 teaspoon fresh lemon juice
1/8 teaspoon kosher salt
1/8 teaspoon black pepper

DIRECTIONS:

1 Combine the Ingredients for the tartar sauce and refrigerate until ready to serve.
2 Crack the egg into a bowl and beat it. Combine panko, and breadcrumbs in a second bowl.
3 Using a fork, place shrimp 1 at a time into the egg, then into the crumbs, then onto a plate in a single layer while breading the rest.
4 Spray the top of the shrimp generously with oil then transfer oil side down to the fryer basket in a single layer in batches.
5 Spray the other side with oil and air fry 400F 4 minutes.
6 Shake the basket and cook 2 more minutes, or until golden.
7 Repeat with the remaining shrimp.
8 On 4 buns, divide the shrimp on each, top with lettuce and 2 1/2 tablespoons tartar sauce on the top side of the bun.

NUTRITIONS:

Serving: 1sandwich, Calories: 352kcal, Carbohydrates: 33.5g, Protein: 34.5g, Fat: 9.35g,

MASALA FRIED FISH

Prep Time: 5 mins   Cook Time: 20 mins   Total Time: 25 mins

INGRIEDENTS:

500 grams karimeen – pearlspot fish (or) fish of your choice

For The Marinade:

2 tablespoon vegetable oil / peanut oil
1 teaspoon apple cider vinegar or plain vinegar
2 teaspoon ginger garlic paste
2 teaspoon chopped curry leaves
1.5 teaspoon red chilli powder
1 teaspoon turmeric powder
1/2 teaspoon black pepper powder
1 teaspoon salt

For The Topping / Tempering:

1.5 teaspoon coconut oil
3 tablespoon chopped shallot / small onion
2 sprigs curry leaves
6-7 cloves of garlic, crushed with skin
a pinch of salt
1/2 teaspoon red chilli flakes

DIRECTIONS:

1 Take in all the Ingredients listed under marinade and mix them well. Use thick ginger garlic paste for this recipe.

2 The oil and vinegar and the moisture from the ginger garlic paste will be enough to make a thick paste. Add a teaspoon of water if only necessary. Make sure that the masala is thick so it evenly coats the fish.

3 Wash, clean and prep the fish. Make small gashes on the fish with a sharp knife so the masalas can penetrate and season the fish throughout. Be gentle and do not cut too deep. These cuts / crevices will hold the masalas later. So take time and make as many even cuts as possible. This is a very important .

4 Apply the marinade on the fish. Make sure that the masalas are evenly coated. Apply masala in the gashes so the fish gets evenly seasoned.

5 Marinate the fish in the refrigerator for 15-20 minutes.

6 We will now cook the fish in the air fryer. The cooking time will vary depending on the size of the fish. I cooked these in the air fryer for 15 minutes at 200 degrees Celsius.

7 The fish was perfect after cooking for 15 minutes. For bigger fishes, cook for 5 minutes more.

8 Now we will make a topping for the fish. Heat coconut oil in a pan and add in the finely chopped shallots (small onion), curry leaves and whole crushed garlic with the skin. Add in a pinch of salt. Fry for 5-6 minutes.

9 The shallots would have become crisp by the time. Now add in the red chilli flakes and remove from heat. The topping is ready.

10 Sprinkle the topping on the fish and serve hot

CHAPTER 6: APPETIZERS & SNACK RECIPES

CORN NUTS

Prep:
10 mins
Cook:
25 mins
Additional:
8 hrs 40 mins
Total:
9 hrs 15 mins
Servings:
8
Yield:
8 servings

INGREDIENTS:

14 ounces giant white corn (such as Goya®)
3 tablespoons vegetable oil
1 ½ teaspoons salt

DIRECTIONS:

1

Place corn in a large bowl, cover with water, and let sit 8 hours to overnight to rehydrate.

2

Drain corn and spread it in an even layer on a large baking sheet. Pat dry with paper towels. Air dry for 20 minutes.

3

Preheat air fryer to 400 degrees F (200 degrees C).

4

Place corn in a large bowl. Add oil and salt. Stir until evenly coated.

5

Place corn in batches in the basket of the air fryer in an even layer. Cook for 10 minutes. Shake basket and cook another 10 minutes. Shake basket and cook 5 additional minutes and transfer to a paper towel-lined plate. Repeat with remaining corn. Let corn nuts cool until crisp, about 20 minutes.

NUTRITIONS:

225 calories; protein 5.9g; carbohydrates 35.8g; fat 7.4g

WONDERFUL TRUFFLE FRIES

Prep:
10 mins
Cook:
20 mins
Additional:
30 mins
Total:
1 hr
Servings:
4
Yield:
4 servings

INGREDIENTS:

1 ¾ pounds russet potatoes, peeled and cut into fries
2 tablespoons truffle-infused olive oil
½ teaspoon paprika
1 tablespoon grated Parmesan cheese
2 teaspoons chopped fresh parsley
1 teaspoon black truffle sea salt

DIRECTIONS:

1
Place fries in a bowl. Cover with water and let soak for 30 minutes. Drain and pat dry.

2
Preheat the air fryer to 400 degrees F (200 degrees C) according to manufacturer's instructions.

3
Place drained fries into a large bowl. Add truffle olive oil and paprika; stir until evenly combined. Transfer fries to the air fryer basket.

4
Air fry for 20 minutes, shaking every 5 minutes. Transfer fries to a bowl. Add Parmesan cheese, parsley, and truffle salt. Toss to coat.

NUTRITIONS:

226 calories; protein 4.8g; carbohydrates 36.1g; fat 7.6g;

MINI PEPPERS STUFFED WITH CHEESE AND SAUSAGE

Prep:
30 mins
Cook:
35 mins
Total:
1 hr 5 mins
Servings:
20
Yield:
20 stuffed mini peppers

INGREDIENTS:

8 ounces bulk Italian sausage

1 (16 ounce) package miniature multi-colored sweet peppers

2 tablespoons olive oil, divided

1 (8 ounce) package cream cheese, softened

½ cup shredded Cheddar cheese

2 tablespoons crumbled blue cheese (Optional)

1 tablespoon finely chopped fresh chives

1 clove garlic, minced

¼ teaspoon ground black pepper

2 tablespoons panko bread crumbs

DIRECTIONS:

1

Heat a large nonstick skillet over medium-high heat. Cook and stir sausage in the hot skillet until browned and crumbly, 5 to 7 minutes. Drain and discard grease; set aside.

2

Preheat an air fryer to 350 degrees F (175 degrees C).

3

Cut a slit in one side of each sweet pepper lengthwise from stem to tip. Brush peppers with 1 tablespoon olive oil and place in the air fryer basket.

4

Cook in the preheated air fryer for 3 minutes. Shake the basket and cook until peppers start to brown and soften, about 3 minutes more. Remove peppers and let stand until cool enough to handle; leave air fryer on.

5

While peppers are cooling, stir together sausage, cream cheese, Cheddar cheese, blue cheese, chives, garlic, and black pepper in a medium bowl until well combined. Mix bread crumbs with remaining 1 tablespoon olive oil in a small bowl.

6

Spoon cheese mixture into each pepper and sprinkle with bread crumb mixture. Place stuffed peppers in the air fryer basket, working in batches if necessary, and cook until filling is heated through and bread crumbs are toasted, 4 to 5 minutes. Cool slightly; serve warm.

NUTRITIONS:

101 calories; protein 3.6g; carbohydrates 2.6g; fat 8.6g

PITA CHIPS

5 MIN
Prep Time:
15 MIN
Cook Time:
20 MIN
Total Time:

INGREDIENTS:

6 pita pockets
1-2 Tbsp olive oil
1/2 tsp ground black pepper
1/2 tsp salt

DIRECTIONS:

1
DISlice your pita pockets into triangles and add them to a large container with a lid (a ziplock bag will also work!). Drizzle the oil over the pitas and sprinkle in the pepper and salt. Cover and shake relatively gently until all the pitas are nice and coated.

2
Add these pita triangles to the air fryer basket and cook them for 10-15 minutes at 320 F, stopping to toss the basket gently every 3-5 minutes until you reach your desired crispness.

3
Let the pita chips cool about ten minutes before serving. They will crisp up a bit more as they cool, so keep that in mind! Serve them on a giant hummus platter or on their own for snacking! These chips are best served immediately, but leftovers can be stored in an air-tight container in the pantry for up to 3-5 Minutes

BUTTERFLIED SHRIMP WITH PINEAPPLE AND MANGO SALSA

Prep:
30 mins
Cook:
7 mins
Total:
37 mins
Servings:
4
Yield:
4 servings

INGREDIENTS:

Salsa:

1 cup diced pineapple
1 cup diced mango
⅓ cup diced red bell pepper
2 tablespoons fresh lime juice
1 small jalapeno pepper, seeded and minced
2 tablespoons minced red onion
¼ cup minced fresh cilantro
sea salt to taste

Shrimp:

1 cup ice, or as needed
1 pound raw shrimp
1 large egg
⅛ teaspoon cayenne pepper, or to taste
sea salt to taste
2 cups panko bread crumbs
parchment paper
avocado oil spray

DIRECTIONS:

1

Combine pineapple, mango, bell pepper, lime juice, jalapeno pepper, onion, cilantro and sea salt in a bowl; stir to combine. Cover and refrigerate, until ready to use.

2

Set a bowl of ice on the work space.

3

Clean each shrimp by removing the head with a twisting motion. Cut along the back of the shell with kitchen shears or a sharp paring knife, and peel off the shell, removing the legs with the shell. Reserve heads and shells for stock, if desired. Clean away the vein that runs along the back, and cut deeper into the shrimp, lengthwise, toward the tail, but not all the way through, to butterfly the shrimp. Place each cleaned and butterflied shrimp on the ice.

4

Place egg in a medium bowl and stir to combine the yolk and the white. Season with cayenne pepper and sea salt. Spread panko crumbs on a plate, and cover a second plate with parchment paper.

5

Remove each shrimp from the ice bowl and place into the egg mixture. One by one, remove shrimp from the egg mixture and place on the panko crumbs. Pat panko into the top side, then place each shrimp on the parchment-lined plate. Repeat, until all the shrimp are coated in panko. Spray with avocado oil spray.

6

Place shrimp in a single layer in the air fryer with the sprayed side down without touching each other. Spray the top of the shrimp with avocado oil spray.

7

Air fry at 390 degrees F (195 degrees C) for 4 minutes. Carefully turn shrimp and continue for an additional 3 minutes.

8

If 2 batches are required, refrigerate raw shrimp while the first batch is cooking. Serve with pineapple and mango salsa and additional lime slices, if desired.

NUTRITIONS:

318 calories; protein 26.5g; carbohydrates 57g; fat 4.2g

STUFFING BALLS

Prep:
10 mins
Cook:
15 mins
Additional:
15 mins
Total:
40 mins
Servings:
4
Yield:
8 stuffing balls

INGREDIENTS:

1 tablespoon butter
¼ cup finely chopped onion
½ cup finely chopped celery
5 cups stale bread, cut into cubes
1 teaspoon dried parsley
½ teaspoon poultry seasoning
½ teaspoon salt
¼ teaspoon ground black pepper
1 egg, well beaten
¼ cup no-salt-added chicken broth
cooking spray

DIRECTIONS:

1

Melt butter in a small skillet over medium heat. Add celery and onion, and cook until softened, about 5 minutes.

2

Combine bread, parsley, poultry seasoning, salt, and pepper in a bowl. Mix in cooked onion and celery. Slowly pour egg into the bowl with one hand while mixing with the other to ensure that the mixture is evenly coated. Repeat with chicken broth and mix everything until well combined. Divide stuffing mixture into 8 equal portions, roll into balls, and place on a plate. Refrigerate for at least 15 minutes.

3

Preheat an air fryer to 350 degrees F (180 degrees C).

4

Remove stuffing balls from refrigerator and spray lightly with cooking spray. Place stuffing balls into the air fryer, sprayed side down, without touching one another. Spray the other side lightly.

5

Cook in the preheated air fryer for 5 minutes, turn, and cook for an additional 2 minutes.

NUTRITIONS:

167 calories; protein 5.2g; carbohydrates 24g

TORTILLA CHIPS

Prep Time: 10 minutes Cook Time: 9 minutes Total Time: 19 minutes

INGREDIENTS:

6 corn tortillas
1 tablespoon extra virgin olive oil
1/2 tablespoon white vinegar
1 teaspoon kosher salt
zesty cheese
2 tablespoons extra virgin olive oil
2 teaspoons nutritional yeast
1/2 teaspoon smoked paprika
1/4 teaspoon kosher salt
spicy chipotle
1 tablespoon extra virgin olive oil
1/2 teaspoon ground chipotle chili pepper
1/4 teaspoon kosher salt
chili lime
1 tablespoon extra virgin olive oil
1/2 tablespoon lime juice
1 teaspoon chili powder
1/4 teaspoon kosher salt
maple cinnamon
1 tablespoon extra virgin olive oil
1/2 tablespoon maple syrup
1/2 teaspoon ground cinnamon
1/2 teaspoon coconut sugar

DIRECTIONS:

1 In a small bowl, whisk together the oil with the Ingredients for your flavour choice. Brush a light coating of the mixture on both sides of the tortillas.

2 Cut each tortilla into quarters to form triangles.

3 Arrange the tortilla triangles in a single layer in your air fryer basket. (You will need to do this in batches).

4 Air fry on 350F for about 7-9 minutes, or until they start to brown around the edges. (Note: the maple cinnamon chips will take 5-7 minutes).

5 Let the chips cool enough to handle and then transfer them to a wire rack to cool completely. They will get crunchier as they cool.

6 Store in an airtight container at room temperature

SPECIAL LEMON PEPPER CHICKEN DRUMSTICK

PREP TIME
5 mins
COOK TIME
25 mins
TOTAL TIME
30 mins

INGREDIENTS:

8 chicken drumsticks
1 tbsp lemon pepper seasoning
½ tsp garlic powder
2 tsp baking powder
½ tsp paprika
1 ½ tbsp fresh lemon juice
4 tbsp melted butter

DIRECTIONS:

1
Sprinkle baking powder, paprika and garlic powder over drumsticks and rub into chicken skin.

2
Place drumsticks into the air fryer basket. 2 Adjust the temperature to 375°F and set the timer for 25 minutes.

3
Use tongs to turn drumsticks halfway through the cooking time.

4
When skin is golden and internal temperature is at least 165°F, remove from fryer.

5
In a large bowl, mix butter, lemon juice and lemon pepper seasoning. Add drumsticks to the bowl and toss until coated. Serve warm.

NUTRITIONS:

Calories 532
Total Fat 32.3
Sodium 706mg3
Total Carbohydrate 1.2g

www.ingramcontent.com/pod-product-compliance
Lightning Source LLC
Chambersburg PA
CBHW070933080526
44589CB00013B/1492